RICHARD LUNDY

LAS VEGAS TRAVEL GUIDE 2024-2025

Exploring the Must-See Attractions, Accommodations and Itineraries

Copyright © 2024 by Richard Lundy

All rights reserved. No part of this publication may be reproduced, stored or transmitted in any form or by any means, electronic, mechanical, photocopying, recording, scanning, or otherwise without written permission from the publisher. It is illegal to copy this book, post it to a website, or distribute it by any other means without permission.

Richard Lundy asserts the moral right to be identified as the author of this work.

First edition

This book was professionally typeset on Reedsy. Find out more at reedsy.com

Contents

Introduction	1
A Brief History of Las Vegas	1
What's New in Las Vegas in 2024	2
Chapter 1: Planning Your Trip	5
Best Time to Visit Las Vegas	5
Navigating Las Vegas Transportation	6
Visa and Entry Requirements	8
Chapter 2: Exploring Iconic Attractions	11
The Strip	11
Fremont Street Experience	13
High Roller Observation Wheel	14
Hoover Dam	16
Fountains of Bellagio	17
Red Rock Canyon National Conservation Area	19
The Mob Museum	21
Bellagio Conservatory & Botanical Garden	23
Stratosphere Tower	24
Neon Museum	26
Titanic: The Artefact Exhibition	28
Chapter 3: Culinary Delights	30
Joel Robuchon at MGM Grand	30
Nobu at Caesars Palace	31
L'Atelier de Joël Robuchon	33
Gordon Ramsay Hell's Kitchen at Caesars Palace	35
Guy Fieri's Flavortown Kitchen at Linq Hotel	36
Wolfgang Puck Bar & Grill at Downtown Summerlin	38

- Sushi Samba at The Palazzo — 39
- Eataly Las Vegas at Park MGM — 40
- China Tang at The Venetian Resort — 42
- The Heart Attack Grill — 43
- Tacos El Gordo — 44

Chapter 4: Shopping, Culture and Outdoor Adventures — 46
- Unique Boutiques and Artisan Markets — 46
- Museums, Galleries, and Historical Sites — 47
- Hiking, Biking, and Adventure Sports — 51

Chapter 5: Accommodations — 54
- Top Luxury Hotels on the Strip — 54
- Hostels — 57
- Vacation Rentals — 59

Chapter 6: Nightlife — 62
- Bars and Clubs — 62
- Live Music Venues — 64

Chapter 7: Events and Festivals — 67
- Annual Celebrations — 67
- Special Events in 2024 — 69

Chapter 8: Itineraries for Every Explorer — 72
- 7-Day General Itinerary for Las Vegas — 72
- 6-Day Romantic Getaway Plan for Couples — 76

Chapter 9: Practical Tips for a Memorable Trip — 80
- Safety Tips — 80
- Health and Medical Services — 82

Conclusion — 84

Introduction

A Brief History of Las Vegas

Las Vegas, famous for its bright lights and entertainment, has a relatively short but dynamic history. Although it's now known for its glitz and glamour, the city's beginnings are rooted in a completely different environment.

Archaeological evidence shows that Native Americans lived in the Las Vegas Valley for over 10,000 years. The Paiute tribe, which settled there around 700 AD, managed to survive the tough desert conditions.

A major shift came in 1905 when the San Pedro, Los Angeles & Salt Lake Railroad arrived. Land auctions near the railway sparked the development of what would later become downtown Las Vegas. Six years after that, in 1911, Las Vegas officially became a city, with Peter Buol as its first mayor.

Gambling and Nevada have had a complicated history. Gambling was legalised in 1931, but from 1910 to 1931, it was banned. Even so, illegal gambling thrived during this time.

In 1931, the construction of the Hoover Dam (initially known as Boulder Dam) brought thousands of workers to the area. The population boom, combined with the legalisation of gambling, set the stage for the city's growing casino industry. This period also saw the rise of organised crime, with figures like Bugsy Siegel shaping the early days of Las Vegas.

Following World War II, tourism began driving the rapid expansion of Las Vegas, leading to the construction of famous hotels like The Flamingo and The Sands. In the 1960s, the city started distancing itself from its mob-related past by focusing on family-friendly entertainment and building sprawling resorts.

Today, Las Vegas is a global tourist hotspot, drawing millions each year with its wide range of attractions, from lavish shows to fine dining, thrilling theme parks, and high-end hotels. The city keeps evolving, embracing the latest trends and technology while preserving its rich history and iconic allure.

Las Vegas's story is one of transformation, perseverance, and a relentless quest for entertainment. From its humble beginnings in the desert to its current status as a top tourist destination, the city's history continues to unfold with exciting new developments on the horizon.

* * *

What's New in Las Vegas in 2024

Always at the cutting edge, Las Vegas is buzzing with new attractions in 2024. Whether you're a regular visitor or coming for the first time, the "Entertainment Capital of the World" has an exciting array of new experiences waiting to be discovered.

Savour New Culinary Experiences
Top chefs like Wolfgang Puck and Michael Mina are creating inventive

menus at Caramá and Orla in Mandalay Bay. At the Flamingo Las Vegas, Gordon Ramsay Burger offers a taste of the celebrity chef's culinary style, while Pinky's by Vanderpump gives you a chance to try Lisa Vanderpump's signature dishes.

For a more casual vibe, Esther's Kitchen in the Downtown Arts District serves California-inspired fare, and NORMS on Charleston and Flower Child in Henderson offer comforting, relaxed meals.

Immerse Yourself in World-Class Entertainment

The Las Vegas Sphere is revolutionising live shows with its cutting-edge design, featuring a massive curved LED screen for immersive concert experiences. Iconic performers like TWICE, Bruce Springsteen and The E Street Band, The Rolling Stones, P!NK, and George Strait are lighting up stages across the city with unforgettable performances.

Families can also check out Ole Red Play Playground, an interactive entertainment venue inspired by country music star Blake Shelton.

Find the Perfect Place to Stay

The Fontainebleau Las Vegas brings luxury and elegance, while the newly revamped Horseshoe (formerly Bally's) offers a sophisticated yet fun atmosphere.

Explore Beyond the Glamour

For sports fans, 2024 is an exciting year, with the first-ever Las Vegas Grand Prix and the Oakland Athletics moving to town, solidifying Las Vegas as a top sports destination.

A City Leading the Way

Las Vegas continues to lead in areas like security, sustainability, and technology, offering interactive experiences and personalised services that enhance the overall visitor experience.

This glimpse into Las Vegas in 2024 is just a taste of the vibrant adventures that await. Get ready to be swept up by the city's infectious energy, where every turn promises something new and exciting to discover.

Chapter 1: Planning Your Trip

Best Time to Visit Las Vegas

Las Vegas, with its iconic lights and non-stop entertainment, is a year-round destination. However, the perfect time to visit really depends on your personal preferences. Here's a seasonal guide to help you plan your ideal trip:

For Weather Lovers: Enjoying the Perfect Climate

If pleasant weather is a priority, spring (March to May) and fall (September to November) are your go-to seasons. The days are warm and the nights are cool, perfect for exploring the Strip, lounging by the pool, or taking day trips to nearby attractions like the Grand Canyon. Just keep in mind that these are popular times, so expect higher prices and larger crowds.

For Budget Travellers: Scoring Deals and Avoiding Crowds

If you're looking to save on flights and hotels, consider visiting during summer (June to August) or winter (December to February). However, be prepared for extreme summers that bring intense desert heat, and winter can be chilly with the occasional rainfall.

For Event Enthusiasts: Timing Your Trip Around Special Occasions

Las Vegas is famous for its events, so planning around them can enhance your trip. Here are a few highlights:

1. New Year's Eve: Celebrate with spectacular fireworks and a festive atmosphere as the city rings in the new year.

2. Electric Daisy Carnival (EDC): In May, dive into the world of electronic music and dazzling visual displays at this renowned festival.

3. National Finals Rodeo (NFR): In December, experience the thrill of rodeo competitions and the charm of Western culture.

A Few Tips

1. Book flights and hotels in advance, especially if travelling during busy seasons.

2. Mix and match seasons to get the best of both worlds pleasant weather and fewer crowds.

Ultimately, the best time to visit Las Vegas depends on what you want from your trip. Use this guide to tailor your adventure to your preferences, and get ready to enjoy the vibrant energy of the city of lights and entertainment.

* * *

Navigating Las Vegas Transportation

Las Vegas offers a world of entertainment, from its dazzling casinos to must-see shows and attractions. But getting around the city can seem daunting at first. No worries! Here's a guide to help you navigate Vegas' transportation options with ease, making your journey as smooth as possible.

Transportation Options

Las Vegas has a range of transportation methods to fit different budgets and needs:

1. Ride-sharing: Uber and Lyft provide easy door-to-door service, ideal for short trips on or off the Strip.

2. Taxis: These are widely available along the Strip and are great for larger groups or those who prefer not to use ride-sharing apps.

3. Public Buses: The RTC runs buses like the Deuce, which offer an affordable way to travel along the Strip and downtown areas.

4. Las Vegas Monorail: This elevated train connects major resorts on the east side of the Strip, offering a quick way to get around.

5. Free Trams: Some resorts at the southern end of the Strip offer complimentary tram rides between them.

6. Walking: The Strip is pedestrian-friendly, but if you plan to walk longer distances, be mindful of the desert heat especially in summer. Wear comfortable shoes and stay hydrated.

Choosing the Right Mode of Transport

When deciding on your transportation, consider the following:

1. Budget: Ride-sharing and buses are economical, while taxis and the monorail tend to be pricier.

2. Distance: Walking or taking the free tram is great for short trips, but longer journeys or trips off the Strip may require ride-sharing, taxis, or buses.

3. Time: If you're in a hurry, ride-sharing and taxis offer faster alternatives to public transit or walking.

4. Group Size: Larger groups might find taxis or ride-sharing more convenient than taking the bus.

Tips for a Smooth Ride

1. Download Apps: Install ride-sharing apps and the RTC app for real-time updates and easy ticketing.

2. Plan Ahead: Map out your destinations and choose the most convenient transportation option.

3. Mind the Traffic: Traffic can get heavy during peak hours, so plan accordingly.

4. Pre-purchase Tickets: Avoid lines by buying bus passes or monorail tickets in advance.

With this guide in hand, you'll be ready to explore Las Vegas effortlessly, ensuring a stress-free and enjoyable experience.

* * *

Visa and Entry Requirements

Before you can dive into the excitement of Las Vegas, it's crucial to understand the visa and entry requirements for the United States. Here's a breakdown of what you need to know before starting your journey.

Visa Waiver Program (VWP)

For citizens of certain countries, the Visa Waiver Program (VWP) offers an easier way to visit the US. This program allows eligible travellers to stay in the US for up to 90 days without needing a traditional visa.

To qualify for the VWP, you need to meet the following requirements:

1. Citizenship: You must be a citizen of a country that participates in the VWP. A full list of eligible countries can be found on the US Department of State website.

2. Passport: Your passport must be valid for at least six months beyond your intended stay in the US.

3. Electronic System for Travel Authorization (ESTA): Even with a VWP-eligible passport, you still need to obtain an ESTA authorization. You can apply for it online, and it's recommended to do so at least 72 hours before your departure.

Non-VWP Citizens

If your country is not part of the VWP, you will need to apply for a visa at a US embassy or consulate in your home country. The type of visa you need will depend on the purpose of your visit, whether it's for tourism, business, or study. The visa application process is usually more detailed and takes longer than the ESTA process, so plan accordingly.

Additional Considerations

1. Customs Declaration: When you arrive in the US, you'll need to fill out a customs declaration form to declare any items you're bringing into the country.

2. Travel Insurance: While not required, having travel insurance is highly recommended. It can protect you against unexpected events like medical emergencies or trip cancellations.

By following these guidelines, you'll be well-prepared for a smooth entry into the US and ready to enjoy all that Las Vegas has to offer.

Chapter 2: Exploring Iconic Attractions

The Strip

The Las Vegas Strip, a vibrant 4.2-mile stretch, is the heart of Sin City. It's packed with world-famous casinos, luxurious hotels, grand theatres, and lively street performers, creating an unforgettable sensory experience. Whether you're seeking thrilling gaming, top-tier entertainment, or simply soaking up the Vegas atmosphere, the Strip has something for everyone.

Key Highlights

1. Iconic Casinos: The Strip is home to legendary casinos like the Bellagio, Caesars Palace, MGM Grand, and the Venetian, each offering unique themes and an array of gaming options for a lavish gambling experience.

2. Spectacular Shows: From Cirque du Soleil's jaw-dropping acrobatics to captivating magic acts and top-tier comedy shows, the Strip's theatres offer a wide variety of world-class entertainment.

3. Luxury Shopping: Indulge in high-end shopping at the Strip's upscale boutiques, featuring iconic brands such as Louis Vuitton and Chanel, along with luxury department stores like Saks Fifth Avenue and Neiman Marcus.

4. Free Attractions: Take advantage of free attractions like the Mirage's volcanic eruption, the stunning Bellagio Fountains water show, and the animatronic spectacle at the Forum Shops in Caesars Palace.

5. Street Performers: Don't forget to watch out for the talented street performers who add to the Strip's lively and colourful atmosphere.

Getting Around

1. Walking: The Strip is pedestrian-friendly, allowing you to explore at your own pace and take in the sights and sounds.

2. Free Trams: Many hotels offer free tram services along the Strip for a convenient travel option.

3. Taxis and Ride-sharing: For a quicker or more personalised way to get around, taxis and ride-sharing services are readily available.

Planning Your Trip

1. Accommodation: The Strip offers a wide range of accommodations, from luxury resorts to more affordable hotels. Booking early is recommended, especially during peak travel periods.

2. Dining: With options ranging from Michelin-starred restaurants to casual eateries and buffets, the Strip caters to all culinary tastes and budgets.

3. Budgeting: While there are plenty of free entertainment options, it's a good idea to set a budget for activities like gambling to avoid overspending.

The Las Vegas Strip offers an unforgettable experience, with its dazzling lights, lively energy, and endless entertainment, attracting visitors from all over the world.

CHAPTER 2: EXPLORING ICONIC ATTRACTIONS

* * *

Fremont Street Experience

Located in downtown Las Vegas, the Fremont Street Experience (FSE) is a dynamic entertainment district that promises a unique and exhilarating adventure. Spanning six blocks, it's a must-visit for those seeking a different side of Vegas.

Once a busy road for cars, Fremont Street underwent a major transformation in 1994 when it became a pedestrian-only zone. Its centrepiece is the spectacular overhead canopy, which stretches 1.5 miles and is a marvel of both engineering and artistic design.

Viva Vision Light Show

The highlight of Fremont Street is the breathtaking Viva Vision light show. This nightly spectacle features 49 million LED lights synchronised to music and captivating visuals, creating a stunning display that lights up the entire canopy. Visitors are treated to an immersive experience of colour, animation, and sound.

Beyond the Bright Lights

While Viva Vision takes centre stage, Fremont Street offers a wide range of other attractions to keep you entertained:

1. Street Performers: The street is alive with talented performers showcasing everything from music and magic to comedy and acrobatics.

2. SlotZilla Zip Line: Get your adrenaline pumping by flying 77 feet above the crowds on the SlotZilla Zip Line, with options for both thrill-seekers and family-friendly rides.

3. Live Music: Fremont Street pulses with live music every night, featuring performances by local and touring musicians on multiple stages.

4. Gaming and Entertainment: Dive into the action with a variety of slot machines and arcades offering both classic and modern games for all ages.

5. Shopping and Dining: Explore a mix of shops and restaurants catering to different tastes and budgets, from souvenir shops and fashion boutiques to eateries serving diverse cuisines.

The Fremont Street Experience is free and open 24/7, making it an accessible and budget-friendly option for visitors. However, some attractions within FSE, such as the SlotZilla Zip Line and certain dining establishments, may require separate fees.

Fremont Street offers a vibrant alternative to the Strip, packed with entertainment, excitement, and a unique slice of Vegas charm.

* * *

High Roller Observation Wheel

Standing 550 feet above the bustling Las Vegas Strip, the High Roller Observation Wheel offers breathtaking, 360-degree views of the city and its surrounding landscapes. Since its opening in 2014, this impressive structure has been a must-visit for anyone seeking an unforgettable Vegas experience.

A Marvel of Modern Technology

- Once the world's tallest Ferris wheel, the High Roller briefly regained the title after Ain Dubai's temporary closure in 2022.
- With a diameter of 520 feet, the wheel completes a full rotation in about 30 minutes.
- The 28 air-conditioned pods can accommodate up to 40 people each, providing a comfortable and spacious ride.

Unforgettable Moments

1. Daytime Rides: Enjoy vibrant views of the Strip, taking in its iconic landmarks and bustling activity.

2. Sunset Rides: Witness stunning sunsets that paint the sky with a blend of oranges, pinks, and purples, transitioning into the dazzling city lights.

3. Nighttime Rides: Experience the magic of the Strip illuminated at night, offering a captivating panorama of the city.

Enhancing Your Experience

1. Happy Hour Pods: Upgrade your ride with a Happy Hour pod, complete with a bar and a selection of drinks and snacks.

2. VIP Pods: For a premium experience, opt for a VIP pod with plush seating, a private bar, and priority boarding.

Planning Your Visit

1. Tickets: Purchase tickets online or at The LINQ Hotel ticket counter.

2. Location: The High Roller is located at The LINQ, a complex in the heart of the Strip featuring entertainment, shopping, and dining.

3. Accessibility: The attraction is fully accessible for guests with disabilities.

Hoover Dam

Venture just 30 miles southeast of Las Vegas to explore the Hoover Dam, an engineering marvel that stands as a testament to human ingenuity and resilience. This massive structure, built during the Great Depression, continues to captivate visitors with its impressive size and historical significance.

A Monument of Innovation

Constructed between 1931 and 1936, the Hoover Dam rises 726 feet high and stretches 1,244 feet across, serving as a symbol of hope and progress during tough economic times. The dam remains an essential source of hydroelectric power and a vital water supply for the surrounding regions.

Exploring the Dam

1. Visitor Center: Discover the history, construction, and significance of the dam through engaging exhibits and multimedia displays.

2. Guided Tours: Delve deeper with a guided tour of restricted areas, including the powerplant and observation deck, where you can view the turbines in action and enjoy panoramic views of Lake Mead.

3. Observation Deck: Take in sweeping vistas of the Colorado River, Lake Mead, and the surrounding desert landscape.

Exploring Beyond the Dam

1. Lake Mead National Recreation Area: Enjoy outdoor activities like boating, fishing, hiking, and camping in the expansive Lake Mead area.

2. Boulder City: Explore this historic town, originally built for dam workers,

with its vintage architecture and fascinating museums.

Planning Your Trip

1. Opening Hours: The Hoover Dam Visitor Center is open daily from 9:00 AM to 5:00 PM, except on Thanksgiving and Christmas. Guided tours have specific times, so check in advance.

2. Tickets: Purchase tickets online or at the visitor centre, particularly during busy periods.

3. Location: Access the dam via the U.S. Route 93, or book a guided tour from Las Vegas.

4. Precautions: Prepare for hot weather by wearing comfortable shoes and bringing plenty of water.

A visit to the Hoover Dam is a journey into the heart of American history and innovation. It's an awe-inspiring day trip that offers a powerful contrast to the bright lights of Las Vegas, giving you a deeper appreciation of the region's incredible feats of engineering.

* * *

Fountains of Bellagio

The Fountains of Bellagio, a mesmerising spectacle of water, music, and light, grace the entrance of the Bellagio Hotel on the Las Vegas Strip. This must-see attraction is free to the public and captivates audiences with its elegant choreography and artistic brilliance.

A Legacy of Innovation

1. Conception and Creation: Conceived by Steve Wynn and brought to life by WET Design, the fountains were completed in 1998, costing $40 million, making them one of the world's most expensive water installations.

2. Technological Marvels: Spanning an 8.5-acre man-made lake, the fountains feature over 1,200 nozzles that propel water as high as 460 feet. A sophisticated system of pumps, filters, and lights ensures the seamless coordination of each show.

A Harmony of Water and Music

1. Musical Variety: The fountain performances are set to a wide array of music, ranging from classical pieces by Pavarotti to hits from artists like Frank Sinatra and Celine Dion. The musical selection is refreshed periodically to keep the experience exciting for repeat visitors.

2. Synchronised Elegance: Each show is meticulously choreographed, with water jets dancing in perfect harmony with the music, creating a stunning visual and auditory experience.

Experiencing the Enchantment

1. Show Schedule: Performances occur daily, typically every 30 minutes in the afternoon and early evening, with more frequent shows every 15 minutes during peak evening hours.

2. Prime Viewing Spots: Ideal viewing areas include the sidewalks along the Strip in front of the Bellagio Hotel. For a more luxurious experience, several Bellagio restaurants and bars offer outdoor seating with views of the fountains.

* * *

Red Rock Canyon National Conservation Area

Located just 19 miles west of the Las Vegas Strip, the Red Rock Canyon National Conservation Area offers a serene escape from the city's neon lights. Spanning 195,819 acres, this geological wonder features striking red sandstone peaks, canyons, and diverse ecosystems.

Natural Beauty and Adventure

- Geological Marvels: Red Rock Canyon showcases ancient geological formations, including the Keystone Thrust Fault, where older seafloor rock rests atop younger layers. The vibrant red sandstone cliffs have been sculpted by erosion over millions of years, creating a stunning natural landscape.

- Hiking and Trails: With 19 trails of varying difficulty, the area caters to all skill levels. The Calico Hills Trail offers a moderate 2-mile loop with panoramic views, while the more challenging Pine Creek Canyon Trail takes hikers into a secluded canyon.

- Rock Climbing: Red Rock Canyon is a premier destination for rock climbers, with over 2,000 climbing routes suitable for all levels. The Visitor Center provides information and resources for climbers.

Cultural Legacy

Native American History: Evidence of Native American habitation dates back thousands of years, with petroglyphs created by the Paiute people visible in various locations. The Visitor Center offers interpretive programs that highlight the cultural significance of these ancient artworks.

Scenic Drive and Stargazing

- Scenic Drive: The 13-mile scenic drive through Red Rock Canyon allows visitors to experience the area's beauty from the comfort of their vehicle, with stops at designated viewpoints for awe-inspiring vistas.

- Stargazing: As an International Dark Sky Park, Red Rock Canyon offers exceptional stargazing opportunities, free from the interference of city lights, making it an ideal spot for night-time exploration.

Visitor Center and Practical Information

The Red Rock Canyon Visitor Center is an essential stop for anyone visiting the area, offering exhibits on geology, ecology, and cultural history. Knowledgeable park rangers provide insights, recommendations, and practical advice.

Fees and Access: An entrance fee is required for access, with options for day passes or annual permits. The area is accessible via car from Las Vegas, though there is no public transportation.

Remember

1. Stay hydrated, especially in hot weather.
2. Wear sunscreen and protective clothing.
3. Use sturdy footwear for hiking.
4. Practice Leave No Trace principles to preserve natural beauty.

CHAPTER 2: EXPLORING ICONIC ATTRACTIONS

* * *

The Mob Museum

Officially known as the National Museum of Organized Crime and Law Enforcement, The Mob Museum is a unique and captivating attraction located in Las Vegas, Nevada. It explores the complex and often volatile history of organised crime in the U.S., with a strong focus on how it influenced Las Vegas.

Housed in the historic Las Vegas City Hall, the museum takes visitors on an immersive and interactive journey through an era marked by gangsters, speakeasies, and the ongoing struggle between law enforcement and crime syndicates.

Exhibits and Displays

The Mob Museum features a wide range of exhibits that shed light on the world of organised crime. Some key highlights include:

1. Mob's Greatest Hits: This permanent exhibit showcases significant figures and events in American organised crime history, featuring notorious names like Al Capone and Bugsy Siegel, as well as infamous events such as the St. Valentine's Day Massacre.

2. The Law vs. The Mob: This exhibit delves into the conflict between law enforcement and organised crime, with interactive displays, historical artefacts, and engaging storytelling.

3. The Exhibit Hall: A deeper exploration of organised crime, covering topics such as the rise of Las Vegas casinos, Mafia influence, and the evolution of surveillance methods like wiretapping.

4. The Speakeasy: Step back into the Prohibition era and experience the atmosphere of a secret speakeasy. Enjoy handcrafted cocktails (both alcoholic and non-alcoholic) and live music in an authentic setting.

Interactive Experiences

The Mob Museum also offers hands-on experiences that bring history to life, including:

1. Witness Protection Simulator: Experience the challenges of entering the Witness Protection Program by making decisions to shape your new identity.

2. Crime Scene Investigation: Test your detective skills by analysing evidence to solve a simulated crime.

3. Sifting for Evidence: Participate in the careful process of gathering evidence, similar to the work of forensic investigators.

In addition to these exhibits and experiences, the museum provides educational programs, including lectures, workshops, and guided tours, making it a valuable resource for students and history buffs.

Planning Your Visit

- Location: The Mob Museum is located at 313 S. Stewart Ave, Las Vegas, NV 89101.
- Hours: Open daily from 9:00 AM to 9:00 PM, with extended hours on Mondays and Wednesdays until 10:00 PM.
- Admission: Tickets can be purchased online or at the museum, with prices varying by age and group size.

* * *

CHAPTER 2: EXPLORING ICONIC ATTRACTIONS

Bellagio Conservatory & Botanical Garden

Amid the lively hustle of the Las Vegas Strip lies a peaceful retreat: the Bellagio Conservatory & Botanical Garden. For over two decades, this renowned attraction has captivated visitors with its breathtaking displays of flowers, plants, and trees, carefully arranged to create stunning seasonal scenes.

Covering 14,000 square feet, the Conservatory serves as a blank canvas for a talented team of horticulturists and engineers. Each display is meticulously designed, showcasing a vibrant variety of flora, often enhanced with sculptures, water features, and other artistic elements.

The displays change five times a year, reflecting the seasons and special occasions. From the romantic atmosphere of Valentine's Day to the joyful celebrations of Christmas, every exhibit offers a unique and awe-inspiring experience.

Beginning March 2, 2024, the Conservatory will celebrate the Lunar New Year with its "Infinite Prosperity: The Year of the Dragon" display. This vibrant exhibit will feature a majestic dragon, symbolising good fortune and power in Chinese culture, surrounded by a colourful array of flowers and plants. The intricate details and symbolic elements transport visitors to a beautifully crafted, Asian-inspired world.

Sustainable Practices

Committed to sustainability, the Bellagio Conservatory strives to reuse and repurpose plant materials to minimise waste and promote environmental responsibility.

Planning Your Visit

- Open: The Conservatory is accessible 24/7, offering convenient visiting hours for guests.

- Location: The Conservatory is located within the Bellagio Hotel & Casino at 3600 S Las Vegas Blvd, Las Vegas, NV 89109.

Tips for Your Visit

1. Free Admission: Enjoy the stunning displays at no cost.
2. Photography: Bring your camera to capture the beautiful exhibits.
3. Guided Tours: Join scheduled tours to learn more about the design and horticulture behind the displays.
4. Accessibility: The Conservatory is wheelchair accessible.

* * *

Stratosphere Tower

Standing tall at 1,149 feet, the Stratosphere Tower (formerly The Stratosphere) dominates the Las Vegas skyline and serves as a top destination for breathtaking views and thrilling experiences.

A Tower of Thrills and Legacy

Since its debut in 1996, the Stratosphere Tower has claimed its spot as the tallest freestanding observation tower in the United States. It's known not only for its stunning 360-degree views of the Las Vegas Valley but also for its reputation as a hub of adrenaline-pumping activities.

Adventure Awaits: Observation Decks and Thrill Rides

A trip to the Stratosphere Tower isn't complete without visiting its observation decks:

- Observation Decks (Levels 108 & 109): Enjoy sweeping views of the Las Vegas Strip and the desert from both indoor and outdoor observation areas. Interactive displays enhance the experience with insights into the city's landmarks and history.

For thrill-seekers, the tower offers several exciting rides:

1. SkyJump: Experience the rush of skydiving with a controlled jump from the 108th floor.

2. Big Shot: Rocket 160 feet into the air and then freefall back down, defying gravity.

3. X-Scream: Hang over the tower's edge at a daring 45-degree angle for a heart-stopping moment.

4. Insanity: Spin at 64 mph over the tower's edge, combining exhilarating drops with incredible views.

More Than Just Thrills: Dining and Entertainment

The Stratosphere Tower also caters to a wide range of interests with dining and entertainment options:

1. Top of the World: Savour fine dining at a revolving restaurant that offers gourmet cuisine with ever-changing panoramic views.

2. 108 Eats and 108 Drinks: Take a break with light snacks or beverages on the observation deck level.

3. Entertainment: Enjoy live music, comedy shows, and special events that add to the tower's vibrant atmosphere.

Planning Your Visit

Whether you're there for the views or the thrills, the Stratosphere Tower offers a memorable Las Vegas experience:

- Location: 2000 Las Vegas Blvd S, Las Vegas, NV 89104

- Operating Hours: Observation Deck: 10:00 AM – 2:00 AM daily; Thrill Rides: 11:00 AM – 1:00 AM daily (hours may vary seasonally)

- Admission: Tickets available online or at the tower, with separate options for the observation deck and thrill rides.

* * *

Neon Museum

The Neon Museum, a beloved non-profit organisation, preserves the rich neon legacy of Las Vegas by safeguarding and showcasing the city's iconic signs.

Exploring the Neon Boneyard

- Location: 770 Las Vegas Blvd N, Las Vegas, NV 89101
- Opening Hours: Daytime Admission (self-guided): 9:00 AM – 4:00 PM (daily)
- Daytime Admission + Guided Tour: Tours run daily at various times

- (reservations recommended)
- Evening Admission (self-guided): Thursday - Sunday, 6:00 PM - 10:00 PM (seasonal)
- Admission: Tickets required, available online or at the museum's visitor centre.

The museum's centrepiece is the Neon Boneyard, an outdoor exhibit featuring over 250 historic neon signs. From legendary casinos like Stardust to lesser-known local businesses, these signs offer a colourful glimpse into Las Vegas' storied past.

Brilliant! Experience

Step into **Brilliant!,** an immersive audiovisual experience that uses augmented reality and 3D sound to bring the Boneyard's signs back to life, illuminating their history with vibrant colours and soundscapes.

Beyond the Boneyard

1. La Concha Visitors' Center: Learn about the museum and its exhibits inside the restored lobby of the historic La Concha Motel.

2. Educational Programs: Participate in workshops and sessions that explore the artistry and history of neon signs.

3. Special Events: Attend lectures, film screenings, and unique photo opportunities throughout the year that provide more ways to engage with Las Vegas' neon history.

Planning Your Visit

1. Guided Tours: Dive deeper into the history and significance of the neon signs with informative guided tours, which are highly recommended for a fuller experience.

2. Nighttime Visits: Experience the Boneyard's signs glowing in the evening, offering a unique ambiance and perspective.

3. Photography: Capture the vibrant colours and history of the signs, with special photography packages available at the museum.

* * *

Titanic: The Artefact Exhibition

Discover the compelling history of the RMS Titanic at Titanic: The Artefact Exhibition, situated within the Luxor Hotel & Casino in Las Vegas. This permanent exhibition offers a deep dive into the ship's storied past through genuine artefacts, detailed room recreations, and personal stories.

What You'll Find

1. Over 250 Authentic Artefacts: Explore a range of recovered items, including luggage, china, floor tiles, and even an unopened bottle of champagne from 1900.

2. Life-Sized Room Reproductions: Experience the grandeur of the Titanic with accurate recreations of spaces such as the First-Class Grand Staircase, the Verandah Café, and a Third-Class cabin.

3. Interactive Exhibits: Engage with multimedia presentations and hands-on displays that shed light on the ship's construction, its ill-fated voyage, and the lives of its passengers and crew.

4. Personal Narratives: Delve into the human stories behind the tragedy, featuring accounts of passengers, crew members, and notable figures like

Benjamin Guggenheim and Margaret "Molly" Brown.

Visitor Information

1. Tour Duration: Allow about 1-2 hours to fully explore the exhibition.

2. Guided Tours: Optional guided tours are available for a more detailed experience, providing expert commentary and historical insights.

3. Suitable for All Ages: Although the exhibition includes sensitive topics, it is appropriate for all ages. Parental discretion is advised.

4. Tickets: Tickets can be purchased online or at the Luxor Hotel & Casino.

5. Opening Hours: The exhibition is open daily, with hours varying throughout the year.

Chapter 3: Culinary Delights

Joel Robuchon at MGM Grand

Located within the opulent MGM Grand, Joel Robuchon stands out as a beacon of French culinary excellence in Las Vegas. Named after the legendary chef, this prestigious restaurant offers an exceptional fine-dining experience, transporting guests to the heart of Parisian cuisine.

Chef Joël Robuchon, often hailed as the "Chef of the Century," transformed modern French cooking. Known for his meticulous techniques, dedication to fresh, seasonal ingredients, and relentless pursuit of perfection, his culinary legacy is evident in his restaurants worldwide, including this esteemed Las Vegas location.

At Joel Robuchon, the dining experience revolves around a tasting menu, guiding guests through a carefully curated selection of the chef's signature dishes and modern interpretations of French classics. The menu changes with the seasons, ensuring only the freshest, most vibrant ingredients are used.

Here's a preview of the gourmet offerings

1. Amuse-bouche: A delightful assortment of small bites to awaken your taste buds.

2. Starters: Tempting selections like foie gras terrine, langoustine ravioli, or

seasonal white asparagus.

3. Main Courses: Impeccably prepared dishes such as roasted pigeon with foie gras, sea bass with Champagne sauce, or lamb loin with black garlic.

4. Cheese Selection: A selection of artisanal cheeses from various French regions.

5. Desserts: Conclude your culinary adventure with a decadent dessert, whether a chocolate soufflé or a fresh fruit tart.

Pricing and Reservations

Prepare for a luxurious experience that comes with a matching price tag. The tasting menu at Joel Robuchon starts at $495 per person, with the option to add wine pairings for an additional cost. Due to its popularity and limited seating, making a reservation in advance is highly recommended.

Location: Joel Robuchon is nestled inside the MGM Grand Hotel & Casino at: Address: 3799 Las Vegas Blvd S, Las Vegas, NV 89109

* * *

Nobu at Caesars Palace

Nobu at Caesars Palace offers a refined dining experience, taking guests on a flavorful journey through Chef Nobu Matsuhisa's innovative fusion of Japanese and Peruvian cuisines.

Location

Conveniently located on the casino floor near the porte cochere entrance, Nobu is easily accessible within Caesars Palace.

Nobu's menu showcases a variety of dishes, each exemplifying the perfect balance between high-quality ingredients and bold flavours. Here's a sneak peek at the offerings:

1. Cold Dishes: Begin with refreshing dishes like spicy miso chips with tuna or scallop (around $20), Kumamoto oysters with Nobu sauce (about $27), or yellowtail sashimi with jalapeño (approximately $32).

2. Sushi & Sashimi: Savour the freshest seafood with Nobu's extensive sushi and sashimi offerings, such as bluefin tuna toro tartare with Royal Ossetra caviar (about $35) or a combination of salmon and yellowtail sashimi (around $51).

3. Signature Dishes: Enjoy Nobu's renowned creations like black cod with miso, celebrated for its rich texture and delicate flavours.

4. Hot Dishes: Indulge in hot dishes like miso-glazed Chilean sea bass or wagyu beef tacos, each highlighting Chef Nobu's culinary expertise.

Price Range

As a top-tier fine-dining destination, Nobu's pricing reflects its commitment to quality and excellence. Plan on spending around $150-$200 per person for a multi-course meal, not including drinks or gratuity.

Reservations

To ensure a smooth dining experience, reservations are highly recommended, especially during peak times and weekends. You can reserve a table through Nobu's website or by contacting the restaurant directly at (702) 785-9750.

Ambiance

Nobu at Caesars Palace offers a stylish and vibrant atmosphere. With its modern décor and attentive service, it's the perfect setting for a special occasion or a memorable night out with loved ones.

* * *

L'Atelier de Joël Robuchon

Experience a slice of Parisian cuisine in the heart of Las Vegas at L'Atelier de Joël Robuchon. This elegant yet cozy restaurant offers a more casual and accessible option compared to its Michelin-starred counterpart, Joel Robuchon at MGM Grand, while still upholding the impeccable culinary standards of the late Chef Joël Robuchon.

True to its name, which translates to "workshop" in French, L'Atelier offers a unique dining experience where guests can sit at the counter and watch chefs expertly craft each dish in front of them.

What to Expect

1. Tasting Menus: L'Atelier features a prix fixe tasting menu that changes with the seasons, showcasing Chef Robuchon's signature French cuisine with a modern twist.

2. À La Carte Options: Alongside the tasting menu, a selection of à la carte dishes allows diners to create a personalised dining experience.

3. Focus on Fresh, Seasonal Ingredients: The restaurant prioritises fresh,

locally sourced ingredients whenever possible, ensuring a vibrant and flavorful meal.

Price Range

L'Atelier offers a more approachable price point compared to its three-Michelin-starred sibling, but it remains a fine-dining destination. Expect moderately high prices.

- **Tasting Menus**: Plan to spend around $150-$200 per person for a multi-course tasting experience.

- **À La Carte:** Individual dishes range from $40-$80, with appetisers on the lower end and main courses on the higher end.

Location

L'Atelier de Joël Robuchon is located within the MGM Grand Hotel & Casino: Address: 3799 Las Vegas Blvd S, Las Vegas, NV 89109

Reservations

Due to its popularity, reservations are highly recommended. You can book your table online through the MGM Grand website or by calling the restaurant at (702) 891-7358.

Dress Code

While there's no formal dress code, smart casual attire is suggested. Think polished jeans or trousers with a collared shirt or chic blouse.

* * *

Gordon Ramsay Hell's Kitchen at Caesars Palace

Las Vegas is home to a wide variety of unique dining experiences, and Gordon Ramsay Hell's Kitchen at Caesars Palace stands out for those seeking both a meal and entertainment. Inspired by the famous reality TV show, this restaurant immerses guests in the atmosphere of the iconic red and blue kitchens while serving dishes crafted by Chef Ramsay himself.

What to Expect

1. Atmosphere: Feel the excitement of Hell's Kitchen as you dine surrounded by the vibrant energy of the red and blue team kitchens, visible from the dining area, adding a touch of drama to your meal.

2. Menu: The menu features a mix of British and American cuisine, highlighting Chef Ramsay's bold style. Dishes range from appetisers like pan-seared scallops and steak tartare to mains such as crispy skin salmon and dry-aged New York strip, all prepared with fresh, seasonal ingredients.

3. Prix Fixe Options: For a curated experience, consider the Prix Fixe menus offered at lunch and dinner, with Chef Ramsay's signature dishes priced from $85 for a three-course lunch to $135 for a five-course dinner.

4. À La Carte: Customise your dining experience with the à la carte menu, featuring appetisers from $22.95 to $32.95, and main courses starting at $39.95, reaching up to $84.95 for premium steaks.

Location

Gordon Ramsay Hell's Kitchen is located at Caesars Palace:
Address: 3570 S Las Vegas Blvd, Las Vegas, NV 89109

Reservations

Reservations are strongly recommended, especially during peak times. You can secure your table online via the Caesars Palace website or by calling (702)

731-7373.

Additional Tips

1. Dress Code: While there's no formal dress code, smart casual attire is recommended for a comfortable dining experience.

2. Valet Parking: Caesars Palace offers valet parking, with validation available for restaurant guests.

3. Special Occasions: If you're celebrating something special, let the restaurant know when making your reservation, and they may add a personalised touch to your dining experience.

Gordon Ramsay Hell's Kitchen at Caesars Palace offers a unique blend of delicious cuisine and the high-energy vibe of the famous TV show. With its diverse menu, attentive service, and lively atmosphere, it's a must-visit for fans of Chef Ramsay and anyone seeking an unforgettable dining experience in Las Vegas.

* * *

Guy Fieri's Flavortown Kitchen at Linq Hotel

Step into Guy Fieri's Flavortown Kitchen & Bar at the Linq Hotel in Las Vegas and embark on a vibrant culinary adventure. The restaurant offers a lively, casual atmosphere adorned with memorabilia celebrating Guy Fieri's signature style. Enjoy the energy of the open kitchen where chefs bring to life each dish with that unmistakable "Flavortown flair."

What to Try

1. Appetisers: Start with the indulgent Trash Can Nachos, a mountain of tortilla chips loaded with pulled pork, queso cheese, and other tasty toppings. Or try the Donkey Sauce Wings, glazed with Guy's famous tangy-sweet sauce. Appetisers generally range from $15 to $25.

2. Main Courses: Dive into the Mayor of Flavortown Burger, featuring a wagyu beef patty topped with donkey sauce, cheese, and onion rings. For a different twist, try the Triple T (Trash Talkin' Turkey) Burger with smoked turkey, applewood bacon, and chipotle mayo. Main courses are priced between $20 and $35.

3. Shareable Plates: Bring your friends along to share the "Knuckle Sandwich" Chicken Fried Steak, served with gravy, mashed potatoes, and green beans. Shareable plates are priced from $30 to $40.

Beyond the Food

The restaurant offers an extensive beverage menu with signature cocktails, craft beers, and a wide selection of wines to elevate your dining experience.

Location and Hours

Guy Fieri's Flavortown Kitchen & Bar is located at:
The Linq Hotel: 3535 Las Vegas Blvd. South, Las Vegas, NV 89109

Operating Hours

- Sunday to Thursday: 11:00 AM – 10:00 PM
- Friday and Saturday: 11:00 AM – 11:00 PM

* * *

Wolfgang Puck Bar & Grill at Downtown Summerlin

Wolfgang Puck Bar & Grill in Downtown Summerlin brings a casual yet dynamic dining experience where Chef Wolfgang Puck's California-inspired cuisine takes centre stage. This location marks Puck's first venture beyond the Las Vegas Strip and features a variety of his iconic dishes alongside new culinary offerings.

What to Expect

1. Menu: The menu offers a range of dishes, including Puck's famous wood-fired pizzas, fresh salads, hearty sandwiches, comforting pasta, grilled meats, and seafood. For guests with dietary preferences, a gluten-free menu is also available.

2. Atmosphere: The lively ambiance is perfect for casual lunches, dinners with friends, or celebratory gatherings. The open kitchen design lets diners watch the chefs in action, adding to the vibrant experience.

3. Price Range: Entrees generally range from $25 to $50, while appetisers and pizzas are priced between $10 and $20. Desserts typically fall in the $10 to $15 range. Pricing may vary, so checking the restaurant's website or calling ahead is recommended.

Location

Wolfgang Puck Bar & Grill is located at:
10955 Oval Park Drive, Suite D3, Las Vegas, NV 89135

Hours of Operation

- Sunday to Thursday: 11:00 AM – 10:00 PM
- Friday and Saturday: 11:00 AM – 11:00 PM

Additional Details

    Reservations are recommended, especially during peak hours and weekends. You can make reservations online or by calling the restaurant. The bar offers a range of classic cocktails, craft beers, and fine wines. For added convenience, valet parking is available.

* * *

Sushi Samba at The Palazzo

Step into a vibrant fusion of flavours at Sushi Samba Las Vegas, located within The Palazzo at The Venetian Resort. This renowned restaurant presents a unique blend of Japanese, Brazilian, and Peruvian culinary traditions. With its dynamic and stylish ambiance, Sushi Samba offers an unforgettable dining experience enhanced by stunning art installations and mesmerising projections.

Menu Highlights

    1. Yellowtail Jalapeño: Fresh slices of yellowtail delicately garnished with a jalapeño sauce.

2. Wagyu Churrasco: Succulent slices of wagyu beef grilled over an open flame, offering a taste of Brazil.

3. Lomo Saltado: A Peruvian dish of marinated beef stir-fried with vegetables, served with rice.

Price Range

- Appetisers: $18-$32
- Sushi and Sashimi: $14-$50 per piece
- Main Courses: $38-$80
- Desserts: $12-$16

Location

Sushi Samba is located at:

The Palazzo at The Venetian Resort

3327 S Las Vegas Blvd, Las Vegas, NV 89109

Reservations

Reservations are highly recommended, especially during peak times. Secure your table online through their website.

* * *

Eataly Las Vegas at Park MGM

Eataly Las Vegas at Park MGM is an Italian culinary haven where guests can explore a range of authentic eateries, specialty grocery shops, and a vibrant marketplace that brings the flavours of Italy to life. Whether you're indulging in fresh pasta, seafood, or artisanal cured meats, Eataly offers a little bit of everything for Italian food lovers.

What to Expect

1. La Pizza & La Pasta: Classic pizzas and freshly made pastas from a wood-fired oven.
2. La Pescheria: Fresh seafood dishes and crudos.
3. La Salumeria: Cured meats, cheeses, and antipasti.

4. La Macelleria: Premium butcher shop offerings.

5. Toscana Ristorante & Bar: An upscale dining experience featuring Tuscan specialties and a curated wine selection.

Price Range

1. Casual Counters: $15-$25 for individual pizzas, pastas, or seafood dishes.

2. La Salumeria and La Macelleria: Prices vary, typically $10-$30 per pound.

3. Toscana Ristorante & Bar: Entrées range from $30-$50.

Location

Find Eataly Las Vegas at:
Park MGM
2700 Las Vegas Blvd S, Las Vegas, NV 89109

Operating Hours

- Eataly: 7:00 AM - 10:00 PM daily.
- Wine Shop: 10:00 AM - 11:00 PM daily.
- La Pizza e La Pasta: 11:00 AM - 11:00 PM daily.
- Toscana Ristorante & Bar: 5:00 PM - 10:00 PM, Wednesday through Sunday (closed Monday & Tuesday).

* * *

China Tang at The Venetian Resort

Experience an exquisite fusion of Chinese culinary traditions at China Tang, located within the luxurious Venetian Resort. Created by renowned Hong Kong chef David Thompson, China Tang offers a sophisticated dining experience that masterfully blends historical influences with modern culinary innovation.

Signature Dishes

1. Steamed Whole Fish with Chili, Garlic, and Black Bean Sauce: A fragrant Cantonese dish that showcases perfectly steamed fish enhanced by chilli, garlic, and black bean sauce.

2. Peking Duck: This iconic dish features crispy skin and tender meat, served with traditional accompaniments such as thin pancakes, spring onions, and hoisin sauce.

3. Stir-fried Wagyu Beef with XO Sauce: Indulge in luxurious Wagyu beef stir-fried in a rich XO sauce, delivering a flavorful and refined experience.

The restaurant's ambiance evokes the grandeur of China's Tang Dynasty, featuring elegant decor, live music, and unique performances, such as noodle-pulling shows.

Price Range

China Tang offers an upscale dining experience, with a typical three-course meal ranging between $100 and $200 per person, excluding beverages.

Location

You can find China Tang at:
The Venetian Resort
3377 S Las Vegas Blvd, Las Vegas, NV 89109

Reservations

Reservations are highly recommended, particularly during peak hours. Book your table online via The Venetian Resort's website.

Dress Code
Smart casual attire is encouraged to complement the sophisticated setting.

* * *

The Heart Attack Grill

For an unconventional and indulgent dining experience, visit the Heart Attack Grill on Fremont Street. This notorious eatery is famed for its oversized portions, decadent fare, and hospital-themed ambiance, where diners are treated as "patients" by staff dressed in scrubs.

Menu Highlights

1. Triple Bypass Burger: A towering creation with three beef patties, bacon, and cheese.

2. Quadruple Bypass Burger: An even bigger challenge with four beef patties.

3. Bypass Fries: Deep-fried in pure lard for maximum flavour.

4. Milkshakes: Made with high-fat ice cream and add-ins like butter and candy bars.

Prices are reasonable despite the generous portions, with burgers starting at $6.27 for the Single Bypass Burger and going up to $9.27 for the Quadruple Bypass Burger. Fries and onion rings range from $3.77 to $4.77, and milkshakes are $6.27.

The Heart Attack Grill is also known for its "Wall of Fame" challenge, where diners who finish the Octuple Bypass Burger earn a free meal and a spot on the wall, though the restaurant humorously warns of the associated health risks.

Location

Heart Attack Grill is located at:
450 Fremont Street
Las Vegas, NV 89101

Opening Hours

- Sunday – Thursday: 11:00 AM – 10:00 PM
- Friday & Saturday: 11:00 AM – 11:00 PM

* * *

Tacos El Gordo

Tacos El Gordo is a must-visit destination for authentic Mexican street food enthusiasts in Las Vegas. Since its founding in 1972, this popular chain has earned a reputation for delivering the rich, bold flavours of Tijuana-style tacos and Mexican staples, drawing both locals and tourists to experience its fresh and flavorful offerings.

What to Expect

1. Signature Tacos: Tacos El Gordo specialises in a variety of tacos with meats like spiced pork (adobada), beef head (cabeza), grilled beef (carne asada), pork stomach (buche), and beef gut (tripa). Customise your taco with fresh toppings, such as onions, cilantro, salsa, guacamole, and lime.

2. Other Offerings: Beyond tacos, the menu also features mulas (double tortillas with meat and cheese), sopes (thick corn tortillas topped with meat and fresh toppings), and fries loaded with your choice of meat.

Pricing

Tacos El Gordo delivers exceptional flavours at affordable prices, making it a budget-friendly option for casual dining:

- Tacos: $3 - $4 each
- Mulas: $5 - $6 each
- Sopes: $5 - $6 each
- Fries: $4 - $5 each
- Drinks: $2 - $3 each

Locations

With several locations throughout Las Vegas, Tacos El Gordo is conveniently accessible for taco lovers across the city. Here are the addresses and contact details for their key locations:

- Sunset Rd: 1724 Sunset Rd, Las Vegas, NV 89119 | (702) 476-0684
- E Charleston Blvd: 3325 E Charleston Blvd, Las Vegas, NV 89104 | (702) 251-8226
- Losee Rd: 2657 Losee Rd, North Las Vegas, NV 89030 | (702) 641-8228
- S Las Vegas Blvd: 3140 S Las Vegas Blvd, Las Vegas, NV 89109 | (702) 331-1160

Chapter 4: Shopping, Culture and Outdoor Adventures

Unique Boutiques and Artisan Markets

Las Vegas offers much more than just casinos and gambling. It also boasts a lively scene of unique boutiques and artisan markets where you can discover hidden gems and support local talent:

Fremont Street East

1. The Artisan: A cosy hub featuring over 30 local artists and vendors, offering handmade jewellery, clothing, art, and home décor.

2. Downtown Container Park: A creative space built from repurposed shipping containers, housing shops like Beatitude for bohemian fashion, Sin City Soap for natural bath products, and Simply Succulents for plant enthusiasts.

Arts District

1. First Friday: A vibrant monthly event that transforms the Arts District into a bustling street festival filled with galleries, studios, and pop-up shops.

2. Art Square: A Saturday outdoor market showcasing a variety of artwork, jewellery, and vintage items created by local artisans.

Off the Strip

1. The Market at Greenspun: A farmers' market offering fresh produce, meats, cheeses, and handcrafted goods.

2. Sun City Summer Market: A Wednesday evening market featuring local artisans, food trucks, and live music during the warmer months.

Additional Tips

1. Be on the lookout for street fairs and pop-up markets for more unique finds.
2. Venture beyond the Strip to discover hidden gems and support local businesses.
3. Engage with vendors to learn about their craft and what inspires them.

* * *

Museums, Galleries, and Historical Sites

Beyond the glitz and glamour of the Strip, Las Vegas offers a variety of museums worth exploring:

1. The Mob Museum: Dive into the fascinating and often turbulent history of organised crime in Las Vegas. Interactive exhibits and historical artefacts bring the rise and fall of notorious mob figures to life.

- Hours: Open daily from 10:00 AM to 5:00 PM.
- Admission: $29.95 for adults, $24.95 for seniors (65+), $19.95 for students (with ID), and free for children 5 and under.

2. Nevada State Museum, Las Vegas: Explore Nevada's rich history, geology, and natural beauty, along with the development of Las Vegas.

- Hours: Open Tuesday through Sunday from 9:00 AM to 5:00 PM (Closed Mondays).
- Admission: $12 for adults, $10 for seniors (65+) and military, $6 for children (3-17), and free for children under 3.

3. Zak Bagans' The Haunted Museum: A must-visit for paranormal enthusiasts, this museum features a collection of haunted objects.

- Hours: Open daily from 11:00 AM to 8:00 PM.
- Admission: $26.95 for adults, $24.95 for seniors (65+), $20.95 for children (10-17), and free for children under 10.

4. Pinball Hall of Fame: A haven for arcade lovers, featuring over 200 pinball machines spanning different eras.

- Hours: Open daily from 10:00 AM to 12:00 AM.
- Admission: $25 (unlimited play) for adults, $20 for seniors (60+) and military, and $15 (20 credits) for children under 12.

5. Springs Preserve: This 180-acre preserve blends history, nature, and entertainment with its Desert Learning Center, Botanical Garden, and scenic trails.

- Hours: Desert Learning Center (daily from 9:00 AM to 5:00 PM), Botanical Garden (daily from 8:00 AM to sunset), and Trails (daily from sunrise to sunset).
- Admission: $12 for adults, $10 for seniors (60+) and military, $8 for

children (3-17), and free for children under 3.

Art Galleries in Las Vegas

Though fewer in number compared to museums, Las Vegas does have a few notable art galleries:

1. Bellagio Gallery of Fine Art: Located in the Bellagio Hotel, this gallery features rotating art exhibitions from around the world, showcasing renowned artists and various artistic movements.

- Hours: Open daily from 10:00 AM to 5:00 PM.
- Admission: Free.

2. The Arts District: This walkable neighbourhood at the north end of the Strip is home to numerous galleries displaying contemporary art by local and international artists.

- Hours: Gallery hours vary, but most are open Tuesday through Saturday from 11:00 AM to 5:00 PM.
- Admission: Free.

3. The Neon Museum: An outdoor museum featuring a collection of restored historic neon signs from Las Vegas's past.

- Hours: Open daily from 9:00 AM to 5:00 PM.
- Admission: $32 for adults, $27 for seniors (65+).

Historical Sites

Las Vegas offers a glimpse into its history with several notable sites:

1. Old Las Vegas Mormon Fort Historic Park: Visit the site of Las Vegas's first settlement, established in 1855, and explore the reconstructed fort.

- Hours: Open daily from 8:00 AM to sunset.
- Admission: Free.

2. Atomic Testing Museum: Located an hour outside Las Vegas, this museum explores the history of the Nevada Test Site and nuclear testing.

- Hours: Open Wednesday through Sunday.
- Admission: $25 for adults.

3. National Atomic Testing Museum: This Las Vegas museum offers exhibits and personal stories from those impacted by nuclear testing.

- Hours: Open Tuesday through Saturday.
- Admission: $15 for adults.

4. Nevada Historical Society Museum: Located downtown, this museum highlights Nevada's history, from mining to Native American culture.

- Hours: Open Tuesday through Saturday.
- Admission: $10 for adults.

5. The Las Vegas Sign: Capture a piece of Vegas history with a photo at the iconic sign at the south end of the Strip.

- Hours: Accessible 24/7.
- Admission: Free, though parking fees apply if you drive up.

CHAPTER 4: SHOPPING, CULTURE AND OUTDOOR ADVENTURES

* * *

Hiking, Biking, and Adventure Sports

Las Vegas is famous for its casinos and nightlife, but it also offers a variety of outdoor adventures just beyond the city limits. Here's a look at some exciting options for hiking, biking, and adventure sports:

Hiking

1. Red Rock Canyon National Conservation Area: A quick drive from the Strip, this area features sandstone canyons, ancient petroglyphs, and stunning panoramic views.

- Popular Trails: Calico Hills, Mosaic Canyon, Turtlehead Peak
- Difficulty: Easy to challenging
- Distance: 1 to 6 miles

2. Mount Charleston: Escape the desert heat and hike through scenic forests up to the highest peak in the Las Vegas Range.

- Popular Trails: Fletcher Canyon, Mary Sachs Loop, Griffith Peak
- Difficulty: Moderate to challenging
- Distance: 2 to 8 miles

3. Sloan Canyon National Conservation Area: Experience a variety of terrain, from rolling hills to volcanic rock formations, on these moderate hikes.

- Popular Trails: Petroglyph, Bitter Creek, Telephone Canyon
- Difficulty: Easy to moderate

- Distance: 1 to 4 miles

Biking

1. Las Vegas Strip: Pedal down the iconic Strip and take in the vibrant city atmosphere.

- Distance: About 4 miles one way

2. Lake Mead National Recreation Area: Ride along the picturesque shores of Lake Mead, enjoying views of the water and desert scenery.

- Popular Trails: The Loop, Boulder Basin, Historic Railroad
- Distance: 5 to 20 miles

3. Valley of Fire State Park: Cycle through dramatic red sandstone formations on designated bike paths.

- Popular Trails: Mouse's Tank Road, Rainbow Vista, Arch Rock
- Distance: 2 to 10 miles

Adventure Sports

1. Rock Climbing: Red Rock Canyon is a premier destination for climbers of all skill levels.

2. Kayaking and Stand-up Paddleboarding: Glide along the tranquil waters of Lake Mead for a relaxing experience.

3. ATV Tours: Head off-road for a thrilling desert adventure.

4. Helicopter Tours: Enjoy breathtaking aerial views of the Strip, the Grand Canyon, or the surrounding landscapes.

Chapter 5: Accommodations

Top Luxury Hotels on the Strip

1. The Venetian Resort: Experience the splendour of Venice in the heart of Las Vegas at The Venetian Resort. This renowned hotel boasts spacious suites with opulent decor, romantic gondola rides along an indoor canal, and top-tier dining and entertainment.

- Location: 3355 S Las Vegas Blvd, Las Vegas, NV 89109
- Rates: Starting from $200 per night.

2. Bellagio Hotel and Casino: Famous for its spectacular fountain show and refined atmosphere, the Bellagio is a landmark of luxury on the Strip. Guests enjoy plush accommodations, exquisite dining, and the enchanting Bellagio Conservatory & Botanical Gardens.

- Location: 3600 S Las Vegas Blvd, Las Vegas, NV 89109
- Rates: Starting from $250 per night.

3. Wynn Las Vegas: Indulge in the epitome of luxury at Wynn Las Vegas, where exceptional service, premium amenities, and stunning design promise an unforgettable stay. Highlights include the chic Wynn Plaza shopping area and

the serene Wynn Golf Club.

- Location: 3131 S Las Vegas Blvd, Las Vegas, NV 89109
- Rates: Starting from $300 per night.

4. The Cosmopolitan of Las Vegas: Offering a modern luxury experience, The Cosmopolitan is known for its sleek design, lively atmosphere, and unbeatable views of the Strip. Guests can unwind in spacious suites, explore diverse dining options, and relax on a rooftop pool deck with panoramic city vistas.

- Location: 3708 S Las Vegas Blvd, Las Vegas, NV 89109
- Rates: Starting from $275 per night.

5. Aria Resort & Casino: Aria Resort & Casino merges cutting-edge technology with timeless luxury. From its striking architecture to world-class dining and entertainment, every detail is designed to deliver a remarkable experience.

- Location: 3730 S Las Vegas Blvd, Las Vegas, NV 89158
- Rates: Starting from $275 per night.

6. Encore at Wynn Las Vegas: As the sophisticated sister property to Wynn, Encore offers an upscale retreat with spacious suites overlooking the Strip, lavish amenities, and exclusive dining and entertainment options, ensuring a luxurious stay.

- Location: 3131 S Las Vegas Blvd, Las Vegas, NV 89109
- Rates: Starting from $350 per night.

7. The Palazzo at The Venetian Resort: Part of The Venetian Resort, The

Palazzo is celebrated for its expansive suites and refined ambiance. Guests enjoy premium shopping at The Grand Canal Shoppes, gourmet dining, and a vibrant nightlife.

- Location: 3325 S Las Vegas Blvd, Las Vegas, NV 89109
- Rates: Starting from $225 per night.

8. MGM Grand Hotel & Casino: As one of the largest hotels globally, MGM Grand offers a vast array of luxury amenities, including elegant accommodations, fine dining, and numerous entertainment options, from the famous MGM Grand Garden Arena to the exclusive Skylofts.

- Location: 3799 S Las Vegas Blvd, Las Vegas, NV 89109
- Rates: Starting from $200 per night.

9. Caesars Palace: Embrace luxury at Caesars Palace, where Roman-inspired architecture meets modern elegance. With lavish rooms, top-tier dining, and legendary entertainment like The Colosseum, Caesars Palace offers an unforgettable Vegas experience.

- Location: 3570 S Las Vegas Blvd, Las Vegas, NV 89109
- Rates: Starting from $250 per night.

10. The Mirage Hotel & Casino: The Mirage combines tropical paradise with Las Vegas luxury. Guests enjoy spacious accommodations with spectacular views, top-notch entertainment, including the famous volcano show, and a serene retreat at the Mirage Pool.

- Location: 3400 S Las Vegas Blvd, Las Vegas, NV 89109
- Rates: Starting from $175 per night.

CHAPTER 5: ACCOMMODATIONS

* * *

Hostels

1. Luxor Las Vegas Hostel: Enjoy a unique blend of luxury and affordability at the Luxor Las Vegas Hostel, located within the iconic pyramid-shaped resort. This hostel features stylish dorms and private rooms with modern amenities, plus access to the resort's entertainment, dining, and nightlife.

- Location: 3900 S Las Vegas Blvd, Las Vegas, NV 89119
- Rates: Dorm beds start at $50; private rooms start at $150.

2. Mandalay Bay Resort & Hostel: This upscale hostel within Mandalay Bay Resort offers a luxurious stay at an affordable price. Choose between shared dorms or private rooms, all with a contemporary design, and enjoy the resort's extensive amenities, including pools, spas, and restaurants.

- Location: 3950 S Las Vegas Blvd, Las Vegas, NV 89119
- Rates: Dorm beds start at $60; private rooms start at $180.

3. The Venetian Hostel: Located within The Venetian Resort, this hostel brings the charm of Venice to Las Vegas. It offers spacious, elegantly furnished dorms and private rooms, along with access to the resort's Italian-inspired architecture, canals, and upscale facilities.

- Location: 3355 S Las Vegas Blvd, Las Vegas, NV 89109
- Rates: Dorm beds start at $70; private rooms start at $200.

4. Wynn Las Vegas Hostel: Experience luxury on a budget at the Wynn Las Vegas Hostel, nestled within the prestigious Wynn Las Vegas Resort. This hostel features chic accommodations with modern furnishings and access to the resort's top-tier amenities, including fine dining and entertainment.

- Location: 3131 S Las Vegas Blvd, Las Vegas, NV 89109
- Rates: Dorm beds start at $80; private rooms start at $250.

5. Bellagio Hostel: Sophistication meets budget-friendly at the Bellagio Hostel, located within the renowned Bellagio Resort. Offering dorms and private rooms with luxury amenities and stunning views of the Strip or Bellagio Fountains, guests can experience high-end elegance and entertainment.

- Location: 3600 S Las Vegas Blvd, Las Vegas, NV 89109
- Rates: Dorm beds start at $90; private rooms start at $300.

6. Aria Resort & Hostel: Enjoy sleek, modern luxury at Aria Resort & Hostel, where chic design meets affordability. This hostel offers stylish dorms and private rooms with cutting-edge technology and access to the resort's world-class amenities, including pools, spas, and dining.

- Location: 3730 S Las Vegas Blvd, Las Vegas, NV 89158
- Rates: Dorm beds start at $70; private rooms start at $220.

7. Cosmopolitan Hostel: Stay in style at the Cosmopolitan Hostel, located within the trendy Cosmopolitan Resort. This hostel offers trendy dorms and private rooms with chic decor, plus access to the resort's vibrant nightlife, gourmet dining, and eclectic entertainment.

- Location: 3708 S Las Vegas Blvd, Las Vegas, NV 89109

- Rates: Dorm beds start at $80; private rooms start at $250.

8. Caesars Palace Hostel: Experience the grandeur of Caesars Palace at this luxurious hostel. Guests can enjoy dorms and private rooms with classic Roman-inspired decor, as well as access to the resort's opulent amenities, including pools, spas, and world-class entertainment.

- Location: 3570 S Las Vegas Blvd, Las Vegas, NV 89109
- Rates: Dorm beds start at $90; private rooms start at $300.

9. The Mirage Hostel: Escape to a tropical paradise at The Mirage Hostel, situated within the lush Mirage Resort. Choose from comfortable dorms or private rooms with modern amenities and enjoy the resort's tropical pool, volcano attraction, and diverse dining options.

- Location: 3400 S Las Vegas Blvd, Las Vegas, NV 89109
- Rates: Dorm beds start at $80; private rooms start at $250.

* * *

Vacation Rentals

1. The Cosmopolitan Residences: Enjoy luxury living at The Cosmopolitan Residences, featuring spacious, stylish condos equipped with modern amenities. Revel in stunning views of the Strip and easy access to world-class dining, entertainment, and gaming options.

- Location: 3708 Las Vegas Boulevard South, Las Vegas, NV 89109
- Rates: Starting from $300 per night.

2. Vdara Hotel & Spa Condos: Unwind in contemporary elegance at Vdara Hotel & Spa Condos, offering well-appointed suites with kitchenettes and panoramic city views. Relax at the on-site spa or explore nearby attractions.

- Location: 2600 West Harmon Avenue, Las Vegas, NV 89109
- Rates: Starting from $250 per night.

3. The Signature at MGM Grand: Indulge in upscale comfort at The Signature at MGM Grand, with luxurious suites featuring private balconies and access to exclusive pools and lounges. The Strip's excitement is just steps away.

- Location: 145 East Harmon Avenue, Las Vegas, NV 89109
- Rates: Starting from $200 per night.

4. Palms Place Hotel and Spa: Escape the hustle of the Strip at Palms Place Hotel and Spa, offering spacious suites with modern amenities, a full-service spa, and access to the vibrant nightlife at Palms Casino Resort.

- Location: 4381 West Flamingo Road, Las Vegas, NV 89103
- Rates: Starting from $180 per night.

5. Marriott's Grand Chateau: Enjoy the comforts of home at Marriott's Grand Chateau, where spacious villas come with full kitchens and separate living areas. Located just steps from the Strip, it offers easy access to shopping, dining, and entertainment.

- Location: 75 East Harmon Avenue, Las Vegas, NV 89109
- Rates: Starting from $220 per night.

Chapter 6: Nightlife

Bars and Clubs

Las Vegas is famous for its dynamic nightlife, offering a wide range of venues to suit every taste. Here's a look at some of the most popular bars and clubs:

High-Energy Clubs

1. XS Nightclub (Encore at Wynn Las Vegas): An upscale venue featuring top DJs, luxurious dance floors, and exclusive VIP sections.

- Location: 3131 Las Vegas Blvd S, Las Vegas, NV 89109
- Hours: Saturday-Sunday, 10:30 AM - 4:00 AM

2. OMNIA Nightclub (Caesars Palace): A multi-level club known for its stunning visuals, diverse music, and immersive atmosphere.

- Location: 3570 S Las Vegas Blvd, Las Vegas, NV 89109
- Hours: Varies, typically Thursday-Sunday

3. Marquee Nightclub & Dayclub (The Cosmopolitan of Las Vegas): Popular for its indoor/outdoor layout and themed nights, attracting a lively crowd with

top DJs.

- Location: 3700 S Las Vegas Blvd, Las Vegas, NV 89109
- Hours: Varies, usually Thursday-Sunday

4. Zouk Nightclub (Resorts World Las Vegas): Inspired by Asian design, Zouk offers a vibrant atmosphere with diverse music genres.

- Location: 3000 S Las Vegas Blvd, Las Vegas, NV 89119
- Hours: Friday-Saturday, 10:30 PM - 4:00 AM

5. Drai's Nightclub (The Cromwell): A rooftop club offering stunning views of the Strip, live music, and top DJs.

- Location: 3595 Las Vegas Blvd S, Las Vegas, NV 89109
- Hours: Thursday-Sunday, 10:00 PM - 4:00 AM

Unique and Themed Bars

1. The Chandelier (The Cosmopolitan of Las Vegas): A visually stunning bar featuring a large chandelier, live music, and creative cocktails in an elegant setting.

- Location: 3700 S Las Vegas Blvd, Las Vegas, NV 89109
- Hours: Sunday-Thursday, 5:00 PM - 2:00 AM; Friday-Saturday, 5:00 PM - 4:00 AM

2. Minus5° ICE BAR (The LINQ Hotel): A bar where guests enjoy cocktails in a sub-zero environment surrounded by handcrafted ice sculptures.

- Location: 3545 S Las Vegas Blvd, Las Vegas, NV 89109
- Hours: Sunday-Thursday, 11:00 AM - 12:00 AM; Friday-Saturday, 11:00 AM - 1:00 AM

3. The Dorsey (The Venetian Resort): A sophisticated bar known for its classic cocktails and live jazz music.

- Location: 3355 S Las Vegas Blvd, Las Vegas, NV 89109
- Hours: Sunday-Thursday, 5:00 PM - 2:00 AM; Friday-Saturday, 5:00 PM - 4:00 AM

4. Atomic Liquors: Established in 1952, this historic bar offers a laid-back atmosphere with vintage décor and a wide selection of spirits.

- Location: 927 Fremont St, Las Vegas, NV 89101
- Hours: Daily, 8:00 AM - 3:00 AM

* * *

Live Music Venues

Las Vegas pulses with vibrant nightlife, and live music is a key element of the city's entertainment scene. From cozy jazz lounges to high-energy concert halls, there's something for every music lover. Here's a look at some of the popular live music venues in the city:

1. The Colosseum at Caesars Palace: A luxurious venue that hosts world-famous artists across a range of genres, including pop, rock, classical, and comedy.

- Location: 3570 S Las Vegas Blvd, Las Vegas, NV 89119
- Hours: Showtimes vary based on the event.
- Entry Fee: Ticket prices vary depending on the performer and seat selection.

2. Dolby Live at Park MGM: A cutting-edge theatre offering an immersive live music experience, featuring top-tier artists and captivating shows.

- Location: 3770 S Las Vegas Blvd, Las Vegas, NV 89119
- Hours: Showtimes vary based on the event.
- Entry Fee: Ticket prices vary depending on the performer and seat selection.

3. House of Blues Las Vegas: Situated on the Sunset Strip, this iconic venue captures the spirit of the blues with intimate settings, diverse live performances, and Southern-inspired dishes.

- Location: 3640 S Las Vegas Blvd, Las Vegas, NV 89119
- Hours:
- Restaurant: Open daily from 11:00 AM to midnight.
- Music venue: Showtimes vary based on the event.
- Entry Fee: Cover charges or ticket prices may apply depending on the event.

4. Brooklyn Bowl Las Vegas: An entertainment complex combining bowling, a concert hall, and a restaurant, offering a unique mix of activities and live

music.

- Location: 3521 S Las Vegas Blvd, Las Vegas, NV 89119
- Hours:
- Bowling and Restaurant: Open daily from 11:00 AM to 2:00 AM.
- Music venue: Showtimes vary based on the event.
- Entry Fee: Cover charges or ticket prices may apply depending on the event, with free entry for bowling during certain times.

5. The STRAT: Formerly the Stratosphere, this iconic tower features live music at various venues such as Aces High Bar, PT's Pub, and Vinyl Showroom, each offering a distinct atmosphere and lineup.

- Location: 2000 Las Vegas Blvd S, Las Vegas, NV 89104
- Hours: Hours vary depending on the venue and event.
- Entry Fee: Cover charges or ticket prices may apply depending on the venue and event.

Chapter 7: Events and Festivals

Annual Celebrations

Las Vegas hosts a vibrant array of events and festivals throughout the year, attracting visitors from all over the world. Whether you're into music, food, culture, or just a great party, there's something for everyone. Here's a look at some of the most popular annual celebrations:

Spring

1. Las Vegas Food & Wine Festival (April)

- Overview: A gastronomic delight featuring renowned chefs, wine tastings, cooking demos, and gourmet dinners.

2. Viva Las Vegas Rockabilly Weekender (April)

- Overview: A nostalgic 1950s-themed event with vintage car shows, live music, dance-offs, and retro fashion.

Summer

1. Electric Daisy Carnival (EDC Las Vegas) (May)

- Overview: A spectacular electronic music festival with world-renowned DJs, stunning stage productions, and dazzling light displays.

2. Life is Beautiful Festival (September)

- Overview: A multi-genre music festival that also features comedy acts, art installations, and culinary experiences.

3. iHeartRadio Music Festival (September)

- Overview: A star-studded music event with performances by top artists across various genres.

Fall

1. National Finals Rodeo (NFR) (December)

- Overview: The ultimate rodeo championship where the best cowboys and cowgirls compete for national titles.

Winter

1. Las Vegas PRIDE Festival (October)

Overview: A celebration of diversity and inclusion featuring a vibrant parade, live music, community events, and educational workshops.

2. Las Vegas Great Santa Run (December)

- Overview: A festive 5K run or walk where participants dress as Santa to support local charities.

Additional Celebrations

1. Chinese New Year

- Overview: A colourful celebration featuring parades, cultural performances, and traditional lion dances to mark the Lunar New Year.

2. Independence Day

- Overview: Patriotic celebrations and fireworks displays light up the city on the Fourth of July.

* * *

Special Events in 2024

Las Vegas is always buzzing with special events, and 2024 is no exception. Here are some highlights:

March

- Nicki Minaj Presents: Pink Friday 2 World Tour (March 8th) at T-Mobile Arena.

April

- Garth Brooks Residency at The Colosseum at Caesars Palace.

- Foreigner Farewell Tour with Loverboy (April 1st-9th) at the Venetian Theatre.

May

- EDC Las Vegas (May 17th-19th) at Las Vegas Motor Speedway.

June

- Life is Beautiful Festival in Downtown Las Vegas.

July

- Las Vegas National Independence Day Fireworks on July 4th.

August

- World Series of Poker at the Rio All-Suite Hotel and Casino.

September

- iHeartRadio Music Festival at the Las Vegas Festival Grounds.

October

- Halloween on the Strip where the Strip transforms into a giant costume party.

December

- Las Vegas New Year's Eve celebrations with dazzling fireworks over the Strip.

Chapter 8: Itineraries for Every Explorer

7-Day General Itinerary for Las Vegas

Las Vegas offers a diverse range of activities that cater to all types of travellers, far beyond just its famous casinos and nightlife. This 7-day itinerary allows you to explore the city's vibrant atmosphere and its hidden gems, providing a well-rounded experience.

Day 1: Dive into the Strip

- Morning: Start your Las Vegas adventure by exploring the famous Las Vegas Strip. Begin with a visit to the Bellagio to admire its stunning Conservatory & Botanical Garden, and don't miss the mesmerising Bellagio Fountain Show.

- Afternoon: Walk over to The Venetian to experience a slice of Italy. Enjoy a gondola ride through its indoor canals and take in the elaborate Italian-inspired architecture.

- Evening: Top off your first day by catching a Cirque du Soleil performance, where acrobatics, art, and storytelling come together in a breathtaking show.

Day 2: Discover History and Culture

- Morning: Head to the Neon Museum to see the iconic, restored neon signs that tell the story of Las Vegas's past. A guided tour will enhance your experience with fascinating insights.

- Afternoon: Continue your cultural exploration at the Mob Museum, delving into the history of organised crime in the city. Discover exhibits on notorious mob figures and their impact on Las Vegas.

- Evening: Enjoy a quiet evening with a stroll around Downtown Las Vegas, exploring local art galleries or grabbing a bite at a historic eatery.

Day 3: Embrace Adventure

- Morning: Escape the city and head to Red Rock Canyon National Conservation Area. Spend the morning hiking or biking through the scenic trails with breathtaking views of the red sandstone formations.

- Afternoon: For thrill-seekers, embark on an off-road ATV tour through the desert. Explore hidden canyons and experience the adrenaline rush of navigating through rugged terrain.

- Evening: Return to downtown for the Fremont Street Experience, where a stunning sound and light show awaits under the LED canopy.

Day 4: Explore Outside the City

- Option 1: Grand Canyon Day Trip – Take a full-day tour to the Grand Canyon. Whether you choose to hike, take a helicopter tour, or a bus excursion, the awe-inspiring views will leave a lasting impression.

- Option 2: Hoover Dam Tour – Alternatively, visit the impressive Hoover Dam. Learn about its construction and significance while enjoying panoramic views of Lake Mead.

Day 5: Connect with Nature

- Morning: Escape to the cooler climate of Mount Charleston. Explore scenic forest trails and enjoy the refreshing mountain air.

- Afternoon: Visit Springs Preserve, a lush nature reserve that showcases the desert ecosystem. Explore the Botanical Garden, the Desert Learning Center, and informative walking trails.

- Evening: Return to the city and unwind with a peaceful gondola ride at The Venetian, soaking in the serene ambiance of this Italian-inspired setting.

Day 6: Treat Yourself and Enjoy Entertainment

- Morning: Pamper yourself with a luxurious spa treatment at one of the Strip's top spas. Relax with a rejuvenating massage or other spa services.

- Afternoon: Spend your afternoon shopping at the high-end boutiques or relax by one of the lavish hotel pools.

- Evening: Enjoy a gourmet dinner at one of Las Vegas's acclaimed restaurants, then catch a dazzling live performance, whether it be a Broadway show, a magic act, or a concert.

Day 7: Reflect and Depart

- Morning: Spend your last morning leisurely exploring the Strip at your own pace. Revisit favourite spots or discover new ones.

- Afternoon: Capture a memorable photo at the iconic "Welcome to Fabulous Las Vegas" sign.

- Evening: Reflect on your week's adventures in Las Vegas as you prepare for departure, cherishing the variety of experiences and memories you've created.

* * *

6-Day Romantic Getaway Plan for Couples

Las Vegas offers more than just casinos, making it an unexpectedly ideal location for a romantic escape. This 6-day itinerary combines city excitement with relaxation, adventure, and cultural experiences, designed for couples with diverse interests.

Day 1: Arrival & Luxurious Start

- Morning: Check into your luxurious hotel on the Las Vegas Strip, renowned for its breathtaking views, world-class spas, and intimate dining options.

- Afternoon: Unwind with a couples' spa treatment or explore the beautiful Bellagio Conservatory & Botanical Garden, a seasonal display of vibrant flowers and intricate designs.

- Evening: Savour an exquisite dinner at a top-rated restaurant like Restaurant Guy Savoy or Nobu Las Vegas, then enjoy a captivating Cirque du Soleil show such as "O" or "KA" for a magical night.

Day 2: Adventure & Exploration

- Morning: Experience the awe of the Grand Canyon with a thrilling helicopter ride, offering a stunning aerial perspective of its natural beauty.

- Afternoon: Take on a side-by-side ATV adventure through Red Rock Canyon National Conservation Area, uncovering hidden trails and colourful desert landscapes.

- Evening: Delight in a gourmet picnic under the stars at Red Rock Canyon, enjoying a romantic meal in a breathtaking setting.

Day 3: Culture & Entertainment

- Morning: Visit The Mob Museum to dive into the intriguing history of organised crime in Las Vegas.

- Afternoon: Stroll through The Venetian's Grand Canal Shoppes, enjoy a romantic gondola ride, and soak up the charming atmosphere.

- Evening: Discover the city's lively nightlife together, whether at a stylish rooftop bar or trying your luck in a casino.

Day 4: Relaxation & Nature

- Morning: Treat yourselves to breakfast in bed or at a cosy café.

- Afternoon: Escape to a luxurious pool or explore the Springs Preserve, where you can connect with nature and learn about the region's history.

- Evening: Relax with a couples' massage followed by a private dinner.

Day 5: Culinary Treats & Shopping

- Morning: Join a gourmet food tour to taste local specialties and hidden treasures.

- Afternoon: Browse high-end boutiques like The Shops at Crystals or The Forum Shops.

- Evening: Indulge in a Michelin-starred dinner, enjoying fine cuisine and flawless service.

Day 6: Departure & Goodbye

- Morning: Savour a relaxed breakfast before checking out.

- Afternoon: Visit the Neon Museum or take a leisurely walk through the Fremont Street Experience.

- Evening: Say goodbye to Las Vegas, taking with you the cherished memories of your romantic getaway.

Chapter 9: Practical Tips for a Memorable Trip

Safety Tips

Las Vegas is a vibrant city full of attractions, but it's important to stay vigilant and adopt smart safety habits for a smooth and enjoyable experience. Here are some key tips to help ensure your safety:

General Safety

1. Stay alert, especially in crowded areas, and trust your instincts if something feels off.

2. Stick to well-lit, populated areas, especially at night, whether you're indoors or outdoors.

3. Avoid carrying large amounts of cash; use your hotel safe and carry only what you need.

4. Keep your belongings close and secure, particularly in busy spots.

5. Use hotel safes to store valuables like documents, jewellery, and extra cash.

6. Drink responsibly to maintain your judgement and awareness.

7. Avoid sharing personal details or travel plans with strangers.

Specific Situations

1. Set a gambling budget in advance and stick to it, only gambling with money you can afford to lose.

2. Choose reliable transportation options like taxis or ride-sharing services, particularly when travelling alone at night.

3. Be cautious around street performers and avoid anyone who seems aggressive or pushy.

4. Trust your instincts; if you feel uncomfortable or unsafe, remove yourself from the situation and seek help from hotel security or law enforcement.

Additional Tips

1. Memorise the emergency number (911) and consider getting travel insurance for unforeseen events.

2. Dress for the desert climate, with comfortable shoes and sun protection.

3. Stay hydrated, especially in hot weather, and be respectful of local customs and culture.

* * *

Health and Medical Services

Las Vegas offers an exciting atmosphere, but maintaining your health is essential for a memorable trip. Here's a guide to staying healthy and accessing medical services in the city:

Staying Healthy

1. Hydration: The desert climate makes staying hydrated crucial. Keep a reusable water bottle with you and drink plenty of water, especially during outdoor activities.

2. Sun Protection: Protect yourself from the strong sun by applying sunscreen with at least SPF 30 and wearing protective clothing.

3. Footwear: Wear comfortable shoes to support your feet during long walks and sightseeing.

4. Balanced Diet: Enjoy Las Vegas's diverse culinary scene while balancing indulgent meals with nutritious options to maintain your overall health.

5. Responsible Gambling: Set limits on gambling and moderate your alcohol intake to protect your well-being.

Medical Services

1. Urgent Care Centers: For non-emergency situations, visit urgent care centres that offer walk-in services and extended hours.

2. Hospitals: Las Vegas has several hospitals equipped to handle a range of medical emergencies and conditions.

3. Pharmacies: You can find pharmacies throughout the city for medications, refills, and basic healthcare needs.

Additional Tips

1. Travel Insurance: Consider purchasing travel insurance to cover unexpected medical costs.

2. Medications: Bring any necessary medications in their original containers, along with a doctor's note if you're travelling internationally.

3. Emergency Contacts: Keep contact information for your doctor and travel insurance provider readily available.

4. Hospital Locations: Familiarise yourself with the locations of hospitals and urgent care centres near your accommodation for quick access if needed.

Conclusion

Las Vegas, often called the dazzling "City of Lights and Dreams," has captivated visitors for generations with its lively energy, mesmerising entertainment, and endless possibilities. This guide has equipped you with the knowledge to fully experience all that Las Vegas has to offer.

From the iconic sights along the Las Vegas Strip to the hidden gems in the surrounding desert, this city caters to a variety of interests and budgets. Whether you're in search of adrenaline-fueled adventures, luxurious stays, or top-tier entertainment, Las Vegas truly has something for everyone.

But beyond the glitz and glamour, Las Vegas is also rich in cultural heritage, historical importance, and outdoor wonders just waiting to be discovered. So, pack your bags, dive into the city's electrifying atmosphere, and set off on a journey filled with unforgettable memories.

This guide has been your map, leading you to:

1. **Exciting Attractions**: From thrilling roller coasters and dazzling shows to world-class museums and historic landmarks, Las Vegas is brimming with attractions.

2. **Luxurious Accommodations**: Experience unmatched comfort and service at prestigious hotels, offering everything from lavish suites to themed experiences.

3. **Memorable Experiences**: Go beyond the casinos to explore the city's hidden gems, including breathtaking natural scenery, delicious dining, and unique cultural experiences.

As you embark on your Las Vegas adventure, remember these key tips:

1. **Plan Ahead**: Research and budget for activities and attractions to tailor your experience and manage your expenses effectively.

2. **Weather Considerations**: Las Vegas can get very hot, so pack accordingly and schedule outdoor activities during cooler parts of the day or year.

3. **Explore Beyond the Strip**: Discover the city's diverse neighbourhoods, historical sites, and natural beauty beyond the famous Strip.

4. **Embrace Spontaneity**: Las Vegas is a city of surprises, so be open to spontaneous adventures and let the city's vibrant energy lead you to unforgettable experiences.

With this guide in hand and a spirit of adventure, you're all set to dive into the magic of Las Vegas and create lasting memories. Safe travels, and enjoy every moment of your journey!

Printed in Great Britain
by Amazon